Positive Affirmations for Black Kids Volume 2

Thoughtful Affirmations Designed to
Increase Self-Confidence, Instill Self-Esteem,
Grow Resilience, and Encourage Self-Love.
Volume 2

Nia Simone

Copyright

Dedication

This book would not be possible without the love and support of T and P.

Contents

Introduction

Did you know every word, every thought, and every sentence you think and say aloud holds great power? Your words and thoughts are powerful, and they influence how you feel about yourself, how you see yourself, and how you project yourself to others. Fill your mind and body with nurturing, supportive thoughts, and cast away any negative thoughts that might creep in. This audiobook is a collection of affirmations designed to honor your strength, brilliance, and boundless potential. These carefully crafted affirmations are for you, the black child who is both a promise to the future and a testament to a rich legacy that runs deep with history, culture, and accomplishment.

In the pages that follow, you will find affirmations that speak to the heart of who you are and who you will become. These affirmations are more than just sentences; they are seeds. When planted in the fertile soil of your young mind, they have the power to bloom into forests of confidence, self-love, and a strong sense of self-worth that will stand tall against any storm.

For too long, many voices in the world have spun narratives that don't reflect the fullness of your beauty, the depth of your capability, or the height of your dreams. This book aims to change that by being a mirror to show you your true reflection—a reflection of someone who is powerful, good, and worthy of all the good that life has to offer.

As you hear and repeat these words, you will embark on a journey of affirmation. An affirmation is a positive statement that can help you to challenge and overcome self-sabotaging and negative thoughts. When you repeat them often, and believe in them, you can start to make positive changes in your life. It is a simple yet very profound act of self-empowerment.

Let these affirmations teach you to embrace the language of self-love and resilience. They are like the sun that warms the earth: essential for growth. For black children, these affirmations are rays of light, guiding your path with hope and pride in who you are. They serve as a constant reminder that you are not defined by stereotypes or by the challenges you face but by the limitless potential and goodness within you.

This collection of affirmations is designed with you in mind—to lift you up when you feel down, to help you see how smart, creative, kind, and capable you are, even if others fail to see it. With every "I am" and "I can," you are declaring your place in the world, taking ownership of your story, and shaping your destiny with intention and power.

Self-esteem is the armor you'll wear on your journey through childhood and beyond. It will help you face any challenge, embrace your individuality, and recognize the strength you have to rise above any obstacle. Self-confidence is your compass, helping you navigate through life's complexities with a sense of assurance and poise. This audiobook is here to nurture those qualities in you so that you can walk into any room knowing your value does not diminish because of others' inability to see it.

Remember, feeling good about yourself is your right, and it is the foundation from which you can reach for the stars. This book is a daily reminder that you are not alone in your journey. Each page is a friend, a mentor, and a cheerleader, urging you to see the beauty in your melanin, the power in your heritage, and the brilliance in your mind. It's a celebration of the skin you're in, the curl of your hair, the sound of your voice, and the genius of your thoughts.

As you read and repeat these affirmations, picture them as your allies in crafting the story of 'You'—a story that is as expansive as the universe and as unique as your fingerprint. Let these words be the daily bread for your soul, nourishing and strengthening you with each passing day.

This book also stands as a bridge between generations. For parents and guardians, it is a way to engage with young ones, fostering a dialogue that affirms and supports their growth and well-being. For educators and mentors, it is a resource to encourage and inspire, to build a classroom environment that is inclusive and celebratory of every child's identity and potential.

We invite you, the parents, the guardians, the teachers, and the mentors, to use this book as a conversation starter and a learning tool. Engage with these affirmations together with your children. Encourage them to speak these words out loud, to write them down, and to live them. Help them understand the power that resides in their speech and the transformative effect it can have on their reality.

With every affirmation, you will not only be learning new words but also weaving a protective garment for your psyche, one that will repel the cold of doubt and the rain of negativity. This garment will grow with you, adapting and expanding to your ever-evolving story.

This is your book, your mantra, and your magic. Let it both protect you from harm and guide you toward your truest expression of self. You are the protagonist of an epic tale, and as you narrate your journey with these affirmations, remember that you are writing chapters that future generations will read with pride.

Embrace this journey, for it is yours alone—beautiful, bold, and bright. And let these affirmations be the wings upon which you will soar to your destiny.

I recommend that you do your best to make time every day to read and repeat a portion of these affirmations. The best times are first thing in the morning and last thing in the evening before you go to bed. But anytime you can find is just perfect.

Affirmations

Every part of me is a friend I love and understand.

♥

I am strong, capable, and ready to shine.

♥

I celebrate my uniqueness; it's my signature in the world.

♥

My smile is my crown, and I wear it proudly every day.

♥

I am more than a number on a scale; I am full of wonders.

♥

Kindness is my shield, and confidence is my sword.

♥

I am the author of my story, and it's a bestseller.

♥

I build my dreams with the power of my positive thoughts.

♥

I am a masterpiece, perfectly crafted and endlessly loved.

♥

Every step I take is a dance of my own making.

♥

My worth is immeasurable, and my potential is limitless.

♥

Challenges make me stronger and braver.

♥

I am wrapped in courage, tied with wit, and adorned with wisdom.

♥

I am a treasure chest of talents waiting to be explored.

♥

My heart is full of joy that spills into the world.

♥

I am a loyal and caring friend.

♥

I know right from wrong.

♥

I have the power to change the world with my kindness.

♥

Every day, in every way, I am getting stronger.

♥

I am a brilliant student of life, learning and growing every day.

♥

I am an ocean of possibilities, deep and vast.

♥

I have a voice that echoes with the strength of my spirit.

♥

My laughter adds light to the world and joy to my heart.

♥

I respect my body as the amazing companion that it is.

♥

I am a rainbow of possibilities, colorful and bright.

♥

I love myself deeply, truly, and unconditionally.

♥

I am proud of my beautiful skin, just as it is.

♥

My hair is a crown of glory and strength.

♥

I am rooted in the rich soil of history and heritage.

♥

My ancestors' dreams live and breathe in me.

♥

I am the embodiment of resilience and excellence.

♥

My voice carries the wisdom of generations.

♥

I am in control of my emotional well-being.

♥

I walk in the light of those who paved the way for me.

♥

My laughter is a song of freedom and joy.

♥

I am sculpted in the image of greatness.

♥

My potential is boundless, and my ambitions are lofty.

♥

I embrace the magic in my melanin and shine brightly.

♥

I honor my culture by being my authentic self.

♥

My uniqueness is a gift to the world.

♥

I am woven from a fabric of stars and limitless possibilities.

♥

I am a vessel of love and a beacon of hope.

♥

The strength of my will is forged by the fire of determination.

♥

I am a living legacy, a bridge to the future.

♥

I do the hard work that others can't do.

♥

I am fueled by the courage of my convictions.

♥

My heart is a fortress, and my spirit is invincible.

♥

I am surrounded by a community that lifts me higher.

♥

The richness of my heritage is a testament to my inner strength.

♥

My intelligence is a torch that lights the path forward.

♥

I speak my truth with confidence and clarity.

♥

I am the pride of my ancestors and the promise of tomorrow.

♥

I am loved, valued, and filled with the power to make a difference.

♥

I am a beautiful story in the making.

♥

My mind is a garden where big dreams grow.

♥

I am brave, strong, and smart in every way.

♥

My skin is a shade of awesome.

♥

I am loved for who I am, just as I am.

♥

My voice is important, and my words matter.

♥

I am a creator of happiness and a dreamer of big dreams.

♥

Every day, I am learning and getting better.

♥

I stand tall like the kings and queens of my heritage.

♥

I am a bright star in a vast sky.

♥

My smile brings joy to the world.

♥

I am full of ideas that can change the world.

♥

I am worthy of respect and kindness.

♥

My laughter is a sign of my inner strength.

♥

I can achieve anything with effort and determination.

♥

I am a leader of tomorrow.

♥

I am a learner today and a teacher tomorrow.

♥

My possibilities are endless.

♥

I am a living legacy of resilience and grace.

♥

I love the uniqueness that is me.

♥

I embrace the challenges that make me grow.

♥

I am an explorer in the world of knowledge.

♥

I am a vessel of peace and understanding.

♥

I am a joyful celebration of black beauty.

♥

You can only achieve success after many failures.

♥

My confidence shines from within me.

♥

I respect my roots and grow towards my future.

♥

I am not just a number, I am a story unfolding.

♥

My courage is like the lion, mighty and fearless.

♥

I am a tapestry of talent and tenacity.

♥

I embrace positive thoughts and banish negative thoughts.

♥

People look at me and see my confidence and my power.

♥

I respect myself, and others respect me too.

♥

I am a work of heart, creating my path with passion.

♥

I am respectful of elders and a role model for my peers.

♥

I bloom with the strength and warmth of the sun.

♥

I am an artwork painted with the colors of diversity and courage.

♥

My natural hair is a crown of beauty.

♥

I dance to the beat of my dreams.

♥

I am a harmonious melody in the symphony of life.

♥

I soar high on the wings of my aspirations.

♥

I am a river of hope, flowing toward my destiny.

♥

My mind is powerful and full of brilliant ideas.

♥

I am intelligent in a way that is uniquely mine.

♥

I have the wisdom of my ancestors guiding me.

♥

My thoughts create a wonderful impact on the world.

♥

I am a critical thinker and a problem-solver.

♥

I am gentle and kind, do not mistake that for weakness.

♥

I am curious about the world and always learning more.

♥

My potential to succeed is limitless.

♥

I am inventive and resourceful.

♥

I carry the history of a people who are strong and wise.

♥

My creativity is a gift to my community and the world.

♥

I am as smart as I am strong.

♥

Knowledge is my playground, and I play with enthusiasm.

♥

I honor my heritage with my pursuit of education.

♥

I am a natural leader who inspires others.

♥

I do not let negative and mean people into my inner circle.

♥

I excel in my studies because I am dedicated.

♥

My intelligence is a bridge to my future success.

♥

I am a trailblazer, making paths for others to follow.

♥

I am a scholar and a gentle heart.

♥

Every question I ask sharpens my mind.

♥

My eager mind is my greatest asset.

♥

My body is my superpower, and I am its hero.

♥

I am a vibrant thinker and a keen learner.

♥

I am confident in my ability to solve difficult problems.

♥

I have a rich cultural legacy that enhances my smarts.

♥

My learning grows deeper with every challenge I overcome.

♥

I am a beacon of innovation and originality.

♥

I am wise beyond my years and learning more every day.

♥

My intelligence is just one of my many amazing qualities.

♥

I respect the knowledge passed down through generations.

♥

I am capable of academic excellence.

♥

I am deserving of love and acceptance.

♥

I am proud of my intellectual achievements.

♥

I am a quick learner and a wise decision-maker.

♥

My thoughts and ideas are valuable and respected.

♥

I am destined for greatness in all my academic pursuits.

♥

I am equipped with the strength and determination to learn.

♥

My culture enriches my knowledge and understanding of the world.

♥

I cherish my unique perspective and share it proudly.

♥

I am an intellectual champion, winning through wisdom.

♥

My mind is an endless ocean of potential.

♥

I am a living legacy of intelligence and courage.

♥

I am a shining example of the power of education.

♥

I am a strong leader.

♥

I use my smarts to make positive changes in my community.

♥

I am the architect of my dreams and build them with knowledge.

♥

I am a visionary, seeing opportunities where others see obstacles.

♥

My voice carries the insight of a deep thinker.

♥

I deserve to be treated with respect.

♥

I embrace complex concepts with excitement and confidence.

♥

I am an eloquent speaker and a thoughtful listener.

♥

I challenge myself to reach new heights in my education.

♥

I celebrate my mind with every book I read and every question I ask.

♥

I am inspired by the great thinkers of my heritage and strive to honor them with my learning.

♥

My beauty shines from within me, bright and true.

♥

I am thoughtful, kind, and respectful.

♥

I am a dazzling blend of history, culture, and potential.

♥

My skin is a tapestry of strength and splendor.

♥

The beauty of my ancestors blooms within me.

♥

My imagination is great.

♥

I am a valuable member of my community with much to contribute.

♥

My life is a beautiful story that I am writing every day.

♥

I have the strength of my ancestors in me, guiding my way.

♥

I have a brilliant mind and a kind heart united in excellence.

♥

My voice is powerful and echoes with the wisdom of the ages.

♥

I have the power to achieve my goals, step by step, day by day.

♥

I am rooted in the love of those who came before me.

♥

My dreams are heard and supported by the universe.

♥

I am surrounded by a sky full of stars; I shine with them.

♥

I walk with confidence, knowing I am worthy of respect.

♥

The love in my heart is as deep as the ocean and as vast as the sky.

♥

My laughter is a song that brightens the world's melody.

♥

I am a courageous seeker of knowledge and truth.

♥

I am a diamond, precious and unbreakable.

♥

I contribute to class discussions with insightful comments.

♥

My skin is rich with history and radiant with potential.

♥

I am defining my future as a bright and brave leader.

♥

I honor my heritage and contribute to its story of strength.

♥

I am not a stereotype; I am an original masterpiece.

♥

My mind is a library of wisdom and imagination.

♥

I carry the courage of kings and queens in my heart.

♥

I am a force of love and positive change in the world.

♥

The content of my character is my truest measure.

♥

I am the architect of my dreams and the builder of my joy.

♥

My voice is a powerful instrument of truth and kindness.

♥

I rise above limitations to reveal my highest self.

♥

I am breaking barriers with my intelligence and grace.

♥

My abilities are limitless and not defined by others' views.

♥

I am the pride of my ancestors and the hope for the future.

♥

My potential to succeed is infinite and knows no bounds.

♥

I stand tall, honoring the greatness within me.

♥

I celebrate the excellence that runs through my veins.

♥

My confidence is unshaken by ignorance and hate.

♥

I am a reflection of beauty, talent, and resilience.

♥

I am empowered by challenges; they prepare me for greatness.

♥

Every day, I am inspired to create a legacy of success.

♥

I embrace my identity and shape it with purpose and passion.

♥

I am a beacon of creativity and a powerhouse of innovation.

♥

I lead with compassion, intelligence, and unwavering strength.

♥

I am surrounded by a universe of possibilities, and I claim them
with open arms.

♥

My presence is a testament to the beauty of diversity.

♥

I am resilient, turning every challenge into strength.

♥

I am a living legacy, flourishing with each new day.

♥

My hands are capable of building dreams into reality.

♥

I am a work of art, painted with the strokes of greatness and grace.

♥

I am filled with the fortitude and spirit of warriors.

♥

I am a gift to my community, and my potential is limitless.

♥

The rhythm of my steps announces my purpose to the world.

♥

I embrace my identity with pride and joy.

♥

I am a beacon of hope and an emblem of a bright future.

♥

My imagination is a canvas for inventing wonders.

♥

I am a beloved and capable child, growing stronger every day.

♥

I am a masterpiece created with love and purpose.

♥

My eyes carry the depth of stars and stories untold.

♥

I radiate confidence and grace with every step.

♥

The rhythm of my heritage dances in my smile.

♥

I am wrapped in the glow of my rich heritage.

♥

My hair weaves the tales of my glorious lineage.

♥

I carry the elegance of the earth in my being.

♥

I am a canvas of endless possibilities.

♥

My spirit is as captivating as my presence.

♥

I wear my history with pride and my future with hope.

♥

My laughter is a symphony that brightens the world.

♥

I am adorned with the resilience and brilliance of my people.

♥

My presence is a gift to the world, one that I share generously.

♥

I am a unique expression of universal beauty.

♥

My beauty is a story written by a thousand ancestors.

♥

I am a living celebration of all that is beautiful and diverse.

♥

I flourish like a rose in a garden of diversity.

♥

I am grateful for my family and friends.

♥

My skin is kissed by the sun, a hue of divine beauty.

♥

I am the creator of joy and the bearer of beauty.

♥

My beauty defies norms and sets its own standards.

♥

I am a carrier of hope and an emblem of loveliness.

♥

In every language in the world, my beauty speaks volumes.

♥

I reflect the beauty of the world back to it.

♥

I am a bearer of beauty, inside and out.

♥

I am determined and resilient.

♥

I can do anything I set my mind to.

♥

Every feature of mine tells a story worth celebrating.

♥

I am a tapestry woven with threads of grace and power.

♥

I embrace the beauty that comes naturally to me.

♥

I am an expression of divine design and earthly elegance.

♥

My smile is a breathtaking display of joy.

♥

I am crowned with the glory of the stars and the strength of mountains.

♥

I move through the world with a beauty that is innate and empowering.

♥

My essence is composed of harmonious beauty and profound strength.

♥

I am a treasure, cherished, and admired by those who know me.

♥

My beauty resonates with the courage and love of my people.

♥

I am sculpted in finesse, rich in culture, and full of life.

♥

My beauty is as boundless as the sky and as vast as the ocean.

♥

I lead by example.

♥

The melody of my heritage is sung through my beauty.

♥

I am a vision of creativity and the image of dreams realized.

♥

I am complete as I am, and my own company is joyful and suffi-cient.

♥

I attract the right people into my life at the right time.

♥

My worth is not measured by the number of friends I have but by the kindness I hold in my heart.

♥

I am open to making new friends, but I am also okay being on my own.

♥

I am a good friend to myself, and that's a wonderful beginning.

♥

My uniqueness is my superpower, and it draws people toward me
when the time is right.

♥

I am patient with myself as I find the right circle of friends.

♥

Every person I meet has the potential to become a friend.

♥

I am becoming more confident in myself every day, which makes
me a magnet for true friendship.

♥

I add value to others' lives just by being me.

♥

I choose to embrace the adventures that come with meeting new
people.

♥

I am worthy of friendship and give friendship uniquely.

♥

Being alone sometimes gives me strength and teaches me about myself.

♥

I have a lot to offer as a friend, even if I haven't met the right friends yet.

♥

My solo journey is just as enriching as one shared with others.

♥

I am building a relationship with myself that will be the foundation for all other relationships.

♥

I can be both a solitary wanderer and a loyal friend.

♥

Confidence grows in me with each new day.

♥

I am learning to love myself more, which helps others love and appreciate me too.

♥

I find friendship in various forms, and not just in people my age.

♥

I grow and learn independently, preparing myself for future friendships.

♥

I enjoy exploring my interests, which will lead me to friends with similar passions.

♥

My heart is always open to genuine connections, which I will find
in due time.

♥

I am kind, I am loved, and I am enough as I am.

♥

I express my needs and feelings, which is a sign of true friendship
with myself and others.

♥

I am confident in making friends, knowing it starts with a smile
and hello.

♥

I celebrate the person I am becoming, and this draws others to me.

♥

My solitude is a space for creativity and self-discovery.

♥

I trust the journey of life to bring me friendships that will enlighten and nurture me.

♥

I am a friend to the world, and in turn, kindness finds its way back to me.

♥

Each day, I see the beauty in myself that the world sees in me.

♥

My uniqueness is my signature, and my beauty is its flourish.

♥

I am a declaration of magnificence and a whisper of wonder.

♥

I stand in the light of my truth, and my beauty shines brighter for it.

♥

I am an infusion of wisdom, warmth, and wonder.

♥

People enjoy being around me.

♥

My beauty is the light that never dims, even in the darkest times.

♥

I am as gorgeous as a sunrise and as mystic as the night sky.

♥

The beauty in me is a lifelong journey of self-love and acceptance.

♥

My mind is a wellspring of great ideas.

♥

I stand tall on the shoulders of giants.

♥

My heart is brave; my spirit is boundless.

♥

I am deserving of respect and kindness.

♥

My words echo the wisdom of my ancestors.

♥

I am a legacy of strength and pride.

♥

I choose to speak with love and act with courage.

♥

My potential is unlimited, and my talents are plenty.

♥

I am grounded in dignity and soaring in dreams.

♥

My laughter is a celebration of my heritage.

♥

I do not waste my time with the haters.

♥

I am a masterpiece painted with the colors of greatness.

♥

I have the power to create change in the world.

♥

My hands build the future with hope and skill.

♥

I am confident, capable, and cherished.

♥

I honor my history by being my best self.

♥

My life is a canvas, and every day I paint it with joy.

♥

I am wise, wonderful, and full of curiosity.

♥

My dreams are valid, and my ambitions are high.

♥

I am the pride of my family and a friend to many.

♥

I walk in the truth of my beauty and the rhythm of my culture.

♥

My presence is a gift to those around me.

♥

I am making healthy food choices.

♥

I carry the spirit of heroes within me.

♥

I have a voice that resonates with power and sincerity.

♥

My roots are deep; my resolve is steadfast.

♥

I am surrounded by a universe of opportunities.

♥

Every challenge I face makes me stronger.

♥

I am the future, bright and promising.

♥

I am a joy to behold and a force for good.

♥

My creativity brings new solutions to the world.

♥

I respect myself, and the world respects me.

♥

My skin is a shade of divine, my smile a burst of sunshine.

♥

I am not just learning; I am excelling.

♥

I honor my and follow my moral code.

♥

I am the sum of many victories and countless possibilities.

♥

My courage is my crown, and I wear it with elegance.

♥

I am a leader on the stage of my own life.

♥

My life is a story of triumph and happy discovery.

♥

I am rooted in respect and grown with love.

♥

My character is built with the strength of my conviction.

♥

I am a living legacy full of potential and grace.

♥

My ideas are innovations that the world awaits.

♥

I see every setback as a setup for a comeback.

♥

I am loved deeply and widely by those in my life.

♥

My success is not if, but when.

♥

I am carving a path for myself that is mine alone to travel.

♥

I fill every room with my light and positive energy.

♥

I am a powerful creator of my personal and community narrative.

♥

My soul is filled with the light of a thousand stars.

♥

Every day, I grow more into the leader I'm meant to be.

♥

I am sculpting a world of beauty with my actions and beliefs.

Thank You

I hope you have enjoyed these affirmations. I would love to hear your thoughts on this book.

Many readers are unaware of how difficult it is to get reviews and how much they help authors like me.

I would greatly appreciate it if you could support me and help get the word out to other people about this book.

To leave a review, please either click on the link below or scan the QR code with your phone. I am very grateful for your support.

https://amzn.to/40EyCLL

References

References

Be Happy Human. (n.d.). Affirmations for men. Retrieved August 13, 2023, from https://behappyhuman.com/affirmations-for-men/.

Gratefulness.me. (n.d.). Positive affirmations for kids. Retrieved August 13, 2023, from https://blog.gratefulness.me/positive-affirmations-for-kids/.

Balanced Black Girl. (n.d.). 10 affirmations guide glow up. Retrieved August 13, 2023, from https://www.balancedblackgirl.com/10-affirmations-guide-glow-up/.

Happier Human. (n.d.). Positive affirmations for teens. Retrieved August 13, 2023, from https://www.happierhuman.com/positive-affirmations-teens/.

Living Well Mom. (n.d.). Positive affirmations for teens. Retrieved August 13, 2023, from https://livingwellmom.com/positive-affirmations-for-teens/.

Lyn Loves. (n.d.). Positive affirmations for black children. Retrieved August 13, 2023, from https://lynloves.com/positive-affirmations-for-black-children/.

MentalHelp.net. (n.d.). 140 daily positive affirmations for men. Retrieved August 13, 2023, from https://www.mentalhelp.net/blogs/140-daily-positive-affirmations-for-men/.

NPR. (2022, February 26). Reflecting on the power of affirmations for Black History Month. Retrieved August 13, 2023, from https://www.npr.org/sections/pictureshow/2022/02/26/1080104890/reflecting-on-the-power-of-affirmations-for-black-history-month.

Our West Nest. (n.d.). Morning affirmations and quotes for black women to empower themselves. Retrieved August 13, 2023, from https://www.ourwestnest.com/blogposts/2020/11/30/morning-affirmations-and-quotes-for-black-women-to-empower-themselves.

Our West Nest. (n.d.). Positive affirmations for black kids. Retrieved August 13, 2023, from https://www.ourwestnest.com/blogposts/0/0/6/positive-affirmations-for-black-kids.

Parents with Confidence. (n.d.). 125 positive affirmations for kids to skyrocket strength, confidence, and self-love. Retrieved August 13, 2023,
from https://parentswithconfidence.com/125-positive-affirmati
ons-for-kids-to-skyrocket-strength-confidence-and-self-love/.

Prodigy Game. (n.d.). Positive affirmations for kids. Retrieved August 13, 2023, from https://www.prodigygame.com/main-en/bl
og/positive-affirmations-for-kids/.